# DEALING WITH FRUSTRATION
# BEFORE & AFTER YOUR DELIVERANCE

Edward A. Butler, Jr.

WestBow
PRESS®
A DIVISION OF THOMAS NELSON
& ZONDERVAN

This book is a work of non-fiction. Unless otherwise noted, the author and the publisher make no explicit guarantees as to the accuracy of the information contained in this book and in some cases, names of people and places have been altered to protect their privacy.

Scripture taken from the New King James Version®. Copyright © 1982 by Thomas Nelson. Used by permission. All rights reserved.

Scripture quotations marked (AMP) are taken from the Amplified Bible, Copyright © 1954, 1958, 1962, 1964, 1965, 1987 by The Lockman Foundation. Used by permission.

"KJV": Taken from the King James Bible

Scripture and/or notes quoted by permission. Quotations designated (NET©) are from the NET Bible® copyright ©1996-2017 by Biblical Studies Press, L.L.C. All rights reserved.

Scripture quotations taken from the New American Standard Bible® (NASB), Copyright © 1960, 1962, 1963, 1968, 1971, 1972, 1973, 1975, 1977, 1995 by The Lockman Foundation Used by permission. www.Lockman.org"

Scripture quotations marked (TLB) are taken from The Living Bible copyright © 1971. Used by permission of Tyndale House Publishers, Inc., Carol Stream, Illinois 60188. All rights reserved.

WestBow Press books may be ordered through booksellers or by contacting:

WestBow Press
A Division of Thomas Nelson & Zondervan
1663 Liberty Drive
Bloomington, IN 47403
www.westbowpress.com
1 (866) 928-1240

Because of the dynamic nature of the Internet, any web addresses or links contained in this book may have changed since publication and may no longer be valid. The views expressed in this work are solely those of the author and do not necessarily reflect the views of the publisher, and the publisher hereby disclaims any responsibility for them.

Any people depicted in stock imagery provided by Getty Images are models, and such images are being used for illustrative purposes only. Certain stock imagery © Getty Images.

ISBN: 978-1-9736-2683-1 (sc)
ISBN: 978-1-9736-2684-8 (e)

Library of Congress Control Number: 2018904934

Print information available on the last page.

WestBow Press rev. date: 07/31/2018

I'm the husband of one wife, married July 28, 1984, to the present. I dedicate this book to the love of my life, Dorothy Deanne Johnson Butler, AKA D.D., Baby Face, the best thing that ever happened to me besides the Holy Spirit. God put you on reserve just for me until I was ready for you. You have stuck with me through thick and thin as well as health and sickness. You've been my friend, lover, and confidant. We've shared many things with each other that we've haven't imparted with anyone else.

My wife, you accepted me for who I am and support me. When I shared with you what the Lord had impressed upon me concerning writing this book, you jumped onboard. During this process, you often asked, "Where are you with your book? What are doing about your book?" Thank you for pushing me!

Not only is she my wife, she's also my assistant pastor and first lady of Wonder Working Word Church. She's an asset and not a liability. She's a woman of wisdom and power. We are still in love today. God has kept us even through the toughest of times. We've experienced the good, the bad, and the ugly. My Mother left us a note that I found after she went to be with our Lord and Saviour. "The two of you are well blessed because of your being united. You stick together and God loves and appreciate your unity. Never let anyone turn you or cause you to be divided. God will always bless you; even if you're being tested and tried.

Thank you, babe, for sticking, staying, and walking by my side where God created you to be because he took you from my side. Thank you for the suggestions, recommendations, and input for this book.

# MY FAMILY

Thanks go to my daughter, Amirah Je'Leta Butler; my son, Tiyari Edward Butler; my adopted son, Nigel Ramon Stewart; and my extended children, Jimmy Aiken and Michael Barnett.

To my one and only remaining sister, Apostle Aleta E. McCurty, you died on May 30, 1974, my birthday. It's a day I'll never forget, but our God put breath in your body and caused you to live again and walk on by faith. God saw fit to leave both of us here to carry on his kingdom agenda. You were my rescuer. (You know what I'm talking about.)

My sister, you were my encourager at so many times in my life. Oh, how I remember the many times you called me to give me a word from the Lord or just to say those sisterly things to her brother. You taught, deposited, and imparted so much into me. I thank God for your life, love, and legacy. I also thank you for having confidence in me and obeying the Lord that you installed me as pastor of the Wonder Working Word Church on July 13, 2013. You are the epitome of woman. You're God's woman. When God made you, he broke the mole.

My brother, Pastor Lawrence Staton, is from the city so nice that they had to name it twice, New York, New York. Thank you for support, love, and prayers. Your sense of humor is beyond words. Keep it. You live what you preach, which is holiness. You are a gift to many through your radio ministry and leadership. May God's best continue to be yours.

My father, Edward A. Butler Sr.; my mother, Jeanette Louise McCurty Butler; my sister, Sharlene McCurty Duckworth; and my brothers, Toi Dion McCurty and

Stan McCurty, are all resting in the arms of Jesus Christ. I wish you all were here to witness and share in this part of my journey.

# SPECIAL THANKS

Special thanks go to Bishop R. D. Edward Goodwin Sr., prelate of 7th Illinois Jurisdiction of the Church of God in Christ; Apostle Leonda Garman, apostle of the Five-Fold Company Inc.; and Elder Remiel Lockwood of RLM Ministries, as well as author, my son in the gospel, nephew, and godson.

To my church family, Wonder Working Word Church, thank you for believing in me and allowing me to serve as your shepherd. I so look forward to our continued journey. It's the fullness of time! You're the greatest church in the world!

# INTRODUCTION

I wrote this book to address an issue I feel affects everyone in the body of Christ as well as the entire world. Consequently I believe it hasn't been dealt with in the body of Christ. As a matter of fact, I've heard it taught and preached that saints and believers don't get frustrated or shouldn't get frustrated.

When you hear those in leadership say it's not easy being a pastor, a leader, and so on, what are you hearing? Or what is that called? When you hear and read pastors, leaders, and laity walking away from a ministry or spouses walking out the door and never coming back, what is that called? We're elated about the callings, promotions, elevations, and appointments, but somewhere down the line, during the journey, something happens that causes us to want to or have thoughts of throwing in the towel and walking away from it all.

We face frustration every day. Let me use a scenario: Our youth who graduate from high school are excited, but now they have the daunting task of applying to various colleges and universities, only to be rejected. College graduates have the daunting task of seeking employment, only to find they can't find opportunities in their specialized degree field. Then comes the repayment of student loans! How frustrating it is to be rejected after achieving your goal and objective or having to settle for a pay grade far below what you are worthy of, but your degree dictates you should be paid double scale.

You get a new cell phone. You're excited. Consequently it doesn't perform like you thought it would. The instructions are very limited. You're not tech savvy. Therefore, the features aren't clear. What's the emotion you begin to experience?

During my time coming up in the church and being active in ministry, I've found that many act and react negatively because of frustration. After hearing how believers acted and reacted before and after their deliverance, I believe the Lord led me to teach a series, "Dealing with Frustration Before and After Your Deliverance."

Hosea 4:6 (AB) says, "My people are destroyed for the lack of knowledge." The word *destroyed* in the Greek means "to be utterly at a loss or in despair." I know in my spirit that God does not want his people lost or in despair before or after deliverance.

I am not dealing with frustration because I have mastered it. On the contrary, I'm dealing with it because I'm mastering it. (I'm a student.) I believe we in the body of Christ need to master it. I believe you can't handle what you're not willing to face. Being filled with the Holy Spirit doesn't mean we're exempt from frustration. Frustration schools me even as I write.

It's my prayer that God enlightens and gives you revelation as we look into this issue called frustration together.

# CHAPTER 1

## What Is Frustration? Is It Found in the Bible?

This book was birthed out of my spirit from a series I taught when our ministry was in the process of raising funds and securing financing to build our church. The Lord gave this series to me to prepare our ministry for the frustrations we would encounter on our journey to build this new church.

You see, we tend to want the product without going through the process. This lesson is imperative to understand because frustrations are commonplace during any journey toward greatness. He brought the plight of the children of Israel to mind. During their time in captivity, they had to deal with many frustrations—fear; pain; anxiety; depression; death of loved ones; physical, mental, or sexual abuse; arranged marriages; hunger; mental anguish; oppression; detachment disorders; a wish for death; a daily brick quota; the process of making cement without straw; and unanswered prayer.

After their deliverance, they had to deal with frustrations—loss of their senior pastor, Moses; the crossing of the Red Sea; false reports ("We can't take the city! There are giants!"); the walls of Jericho; the crossing of the Jordan River; war; the Hittites, Amorites, Canaanites, Perizzites, Hivites, and Jebusites; and the comparison of themselves to other nations. Similarly, our ministry would have to face frustrations even after achieving our goal and arriving at our very own Promised Land.

Frustration also stemmed from the differences between their physical and mental condition. They were physically free; however, even after their deliverance, they maintained their mentality rooted in captivity. This conflict resulted in them finding themselves disobeying God, finding fault with their leader, and looking back to Egypt. What sense would it make for them to go back to bondage when God delivered them? Who in his or her right mind would essentially want to undo a God-answered prayer or return or refund his or her deliverance?

According to Webster's, the word *frustration* means to keep from attaining a goal or fulfilling a desire; to thwart (defeat, prevent, foil, stop, baffle circumvent, hinder, obstruct, disappoint, balk, or outwit); to prevent the fruition of; or to nullify.

First, let me say that you won't find the word *frustration* in the Bible in the way God has me dealing with it. However, you will find *frustrate*. Philippians 4:6 (AB) says the following concerning frustration, "Do not fret (frustrate) or have any anxiety about anything, but in every circumstance and in everything, by prayer and petition (definite requests), with thanksgiving, continue to make your wants known to God." Praying and giving thanks are key methodologies to combat frustration.

You must understand that frustration is a tool that the adversary uses to prevent us from attaining our goal and to keep us from God's purpose in our lives. Romans 8:29–30 (AB) says,

> For those whom He foreknew [and loved and chose beforehand], He also predestined to be conformed to the image of His Son [and ultimately share in His complete sanctification], so that He would be the firstborn [the most beloved and honored] among many believers. And those whom He predestined, He also called; and

those whom He called, He also justified [declared free of the guilt of sin]; and those whom He justified, He also glorified [raising them to a heavenly dignity].

God's purpose for you was not an afterthought. It was established before the foundation of the world. If you allow the adversary to obstruct, hinder, or stop you from attaining that which God has designed for you, you will remain frustrated or in a frustrating situation. Frustration can block your promises in your season of reaping.

Frustration is a trick of the enemy. I'm not saying that we will not get or become frustrated. It is inevitable. However, what's important is that we cope with and work through frustration. Without a process, there's no product. Psalm 37:1–2 (AB) says, "Fret not yourself because of evildoers, neither be envious against those who work unrighteousness (that which is not upright or in right standing with God). For they shall soon be cut down like the grass, and wither as the green herb."

Nothing can happen in your life that is outside the will and control of God. The enemy would have you think that God has left you, no one cares, and not a person understands what you're going through. The devil is a liar! The Bible says, "God never sleeps nor slumbers" (Ps. 121:4 AB) and "The eyes of the Lord are in every place, watching the evil and the good [in all their endeavors]" (Prov. 15:3 AB).

Frustration is part of the process that will get you to where you're supposed to be if you handle it right. Oh yes, you must handle your frustration as well as your frustrating circumstances. They're not going away! Job 5:12 (AB, my emphasis) says, "He *frustrates*, e.g., thwarts the devices of the crafty, so that their hands cannot perform their enterprise or anything of [lasting] worth."

Repeat this, "This that I'm going through, it did not come to stay."

# CHAPTER 2

# Handling Frustration

The way you handle frustration before your deliverance is important. However, many forget that what you do after deliverance (and how you do it) is equally important. Your actions after you've been delivered determine the length of time God may take before he comes through for you again, and it will determine how long you stay in the constant flow of his blessings and favor.

We don't handle frustration in the same manner that those of the world tend to handle frustration. Let's see how the Word says we should address frustration, according to Romans 12:1–2 (NIV),

> Therefore, I urge you, brothers, in view of God's mercy, to offer your bodies as living sacrifices, holy and pleasing to God—this is your spiritual act of worship. Do not conform any longer to the pattern of this world, *but be transformed* by the renewing of your mind. *Then* you will be able to test and approve what God's will is—His good, pleasing and perfect will.

Etymology teaches us that the prefix *trans* means across, through, over, beyond, to, or on the other side of. I've been through some trials that were indeed frustrating, and they helped shape me and brought forth a new me. I was transformed and became an improved version of myself.

There are frustrations with being both poor or rich. Many people believe that their frustrations would be nonexistent if they had more money. That is not the case.

Although Ecclesiastes 10:19 (KJV) says that money answers all things, frustration will nevertheless rear its ugly head. Being poor has its frustrations, for example, not having enough or none at all. You're in Christendom, yet you see the wicked lacking nothing and prospering while you struggle, trying to make ends meet.

Let's face it. Many are living from paycheck to paycheck. But being in this condition is not always due to a lack of managing finances. It can be a consequence of other things, such as divorce, a downsize of jobs, or illness. And the list goes on. But a promise is found in Psalm 34:10 (AB), "The young lions lack [food] and grow hungry, But they who seek the Lord will not lack any good thing."

We must first do what Peter said in 1 Peter 5:7 (KJV), "Casting all your care upon Him for He cares for you." The word *casting* in the passage of scripture means to roll away or throw upon. When you roll away your problems, concerns, issues, worries, and burdens or throw them upon him, you don't go back and get them.

Sometimes we become frustrated with God because we feel he is not moving or working fast enough. We love helping God. But guess what, my friend? God does not need our help. When we try to help God, we mess up or make a mess of everything.

Look at Abraham and Sarah. God promised them a child, but out of frustration, Sarah felt she was too old to have one. So she thought she would help God out, telling Abraham to go in and lay with Hagar. And out of that relationship came Ishmael. If God has given you a word, don't let frustration rule your emotions and decisions. Frustration will cause you to make wrong decisions that will have long-lasting effects. Abraham ended up sending Hagar and Ishmael away.

Frustration will cause you to think irrationally. It will cause you to be reactive instead of proactive. As a young adult, I fell into some financial difficulty. One day I received a letter stating that my wages would be garnished because of unpaid debt totaling approximately $550. I became overwhelmed with frustration, and I reacted out of panic, ignorance, and fear. I immediately sought out a bankruptcy attorney due to misleading information that someone I considered my elder provided. (I will later address seeking counsel in a multitude.)

At such a young age, I had no business filing for bankruptcy. But because I allowed frustration and emotion to override logic and rationality, I made a hasty and inappropriate decision, one that affected and stagnated me for about ten years. Hosea 4:6 (NKJV) says, "My people are destroyed for lack of knowledge."

If I had taken the time to think with a sound mind and seek God's direction, the outcome would have been less drastic, and the effects would not have been as detrimental for the years to come. Psalm 37:23 (AB) encourages us, "The steps of a [good and righteous] man are directed and established by the Lord, And He delights in his way [and blesses his path]."

If I would have rationally thought things through, I would have discovered that the company was only going to deduct a certain percentage of my salary each pay period until the debt was settled. In retrospect, the debt would have been settled in approximately two months. My friend, don't sacrifice your future for the present. Proverbs 3:6 AB says, "In all your ways know, recognize, and acknowledge Him, and He will direct and make straight and plain your paths." You see, it is the enemy's plan to destroy you or take you out. But you must affirm, "I'm not going out like that. If God is for me, he is more than the world against me."

You cannot let frustration be the driving force behind your decision-making. If you allow frustration to be the driving force, you will make choices that you will regret later, and it will leave no room for God. That is why our focal verse Philippians 4:6 (AB) says, "Do not fret about anything, but in every circumstance and in everything, by prayer and petition (definite requests), with thanksgiving, continue to make your wants known to God."

Frustration will cause you to miss what God is doing in your life. It will blind you to opportunities for growth, development, and new challenges. If you focus on the new challenges, adversities, or obstacles in a frustrating manner, you may miss God's handy work or come to the wrong conclusion. During a time of my supervisory career, I was responsible for managing what seemed to me a fairly large team. However, as the turn of events would have it, my team ended up being doubled. I was to manage a fairly large team.

Cultivating the talent and teamwork was a constant obstacle at my job. Out of frustration, I immediately concluded that I was being set up for failure. I spent years allowing frustration, stress, fear, worry, sleeplessness, and anxiety to grip my life. Things got so bad that I became afraid to take a day off or even a vacation, fearing what chaos or negative changes would be waiting for me upon my return. I would wake up in the middle of night with cold sweats.

My sleep would be interrupted with nervous thoughts like, *Oh my! I didn't do this, and that wasn't done. Maybe I should have done ...*" I began to question my abilities as a supervisor and a leader, and this doubt also resulted in me questioning and doubting myself as a spiritual leader.

You may ask, "Why didn't you quit?" Well, I made God a promise after being unemployed for nine years that, when he blessed me with another job, I would never walk off another job as long as I lived. Don't let anyone tell you that saints or believers don't have thoughts of suicide. We are human! There were many days where I felt like walking away from it all, taking my own life by going out of the window of the building where I worked.

When you're caught in the grip of frustration, it's hard to focus on God. I know, I know, God will keep you in perfect peace whose mind is stayed on him. Tell me about it. When you're dealing with frustrating situations, sometimes you have to get a song that will help you through the phase you're in at that particular time.

During a particular phase of what I was enduring, certain songs ministered to me: "Seasons," "Restoring the Years," and "You Covered Me" by Donald Lawrence. Then there was "Hallelujah, the Lord God Almighty Reigns" and "Jesus" by Judy Jacobs.

Psalm 98:1 (KJV) says, "O sing unto the LORD a new song; for he hath done marvelous things: his right hand, and his holy arm, hath gotten him the victory." Child of God, I had to get centered. I prayed and asked God to deliver me from this situation. My sister, who was also my pastor, called me and ministered to me. She would say, "I feel your spirit. God is going to bring you out. Hold on. God has not forgotten or left you."

Please understand that God will not always deliver you out of a situation. Sometimes he will deliver you while you're in the situation. For Shadrach, Meshach, and Abednego, God did not deliver them from the furnace. On the contrary, he allowed them to be thrown into the furnace. However, he empowered and covered them so they might endure the fire of the furnace. Daniel 3:22 (KJV) says, "because of the exceeding heat," the men that escorted Shadrach, Meshach, and Abednego were killed. However, the three men themselves were not harmed.

Remember that I stated before, if you focus too much on the challenge, you'll miss God's handiwork and not realize that he is molding and shaping you to the individual that he has declared, predestined, and designed for you to become.

Shadrach, Meshach, and Abednego were delivered while they were in the furnace. He came down in the furnace with the three and took the heat out of the flame. I once preached a message, "Don't Forget about the Fourth One!"

There were times I shared with others who were experiencing the same frustrating dilemmas as I was. I would witness and see deliverance come their way, while I was still going through. This made me have questions for God, "Why haven't you delivered me yet?" It appeared to me that more frustrating events were piling upon me. Sometimes it gets worse before it gets better. Things got so bad that I began to seek therapy and counseling. Frustration was in my home, job, church, and so on. The fire got hotter.

I was advised that I needed to develop tough skin and stop feeling sorry for myself. In my opinion, that was very good advice, but I didn't want hear that during that time. God was answering me, but I didn't have an ear to hear what I believe the Spirit was trying to convey to me. I had to change my focus, and I began to pray, "God, whatever you are trying to deposit and work in me, help me to get it and whatever you're trying to get out of me, take it out of me."

I believe the Lord answered me by taking me to 1 Peter 5:10 (KJV), "But the God of all grace, who hath called us unto his eternal glory by Christ Jesus after that ye have suffered a while, make you perfect, establish, strengthen, settle you." I began to read this passage of scripture daily. Not too long after that, I saw the glory of God manifested.

One morning I began to see deliverance coming to me one situation at a time. It was like a bright light that began to shine on my frustrating situation. Burdens were rolled away, and weights were lifted. I felt my strength coming back to me. Won't he do it?

You see, God didn't take me out of the fire, but he took the heat out of the fire. Glory to God! First Peter 3:12 (AB) says, "For the eyes of the Lord are upon the righteous (those who are upright and in right standing with God), and His ears are attentive to their prayer. But the face of the Lord is against those who practice evil [to oppose them, to **frustrate**, and defeat them]." What the devil meant for evil, God turned it around for my good. God will frustrate the plans of the enemy for you.

In June 2001, I was diagnosed with sarcoidosis, a disease that can affect many organs within the body. It causes the development of granulomas, masses resembling little tumors. They are made up of clumps of cells from the immune system, and its cause is unknown.

I received this diagnosis after several visits to the doctor's office for a persistent dry cough. I would have a coughing attack anytime and anywhere. I would be interviewing potential candidates and suddenly begin to cough. I used cough drops and tried drinking water to stop the cough. At times, I felt like someone was choking me and/or cutting off my air supply. I would even begin to gag as though I had to vomit. Positioning my head a certain way or even laughing would initiate a coughing spell.

My doctor thought I was suffering from allergies, so he prescribed various drugs, along with cough medication, to combat what he thought was the problem. After several visits to the doctor, he took some blood work, and after receiving the results, he referred me to a pulmonary specialist, who conducted a bronchoscopy. They inserted a tiny tube in the nose or mouth. The tube is sent down the trachea and into the bronchial tubes, or airways. The result of the study was the discovery of the granulomas that characterize sarcoidosis.

I was placed on a steroid along with two different types of inhalants to decrease inflammation. While the steroid medication worked, the side effects were nothing nice. I experienced weight gain, swelling, pain in my joints, abnormal blood clotting if I cut myself, decrease in vision, and mood changes.

I asked the Lord why and how I contracted this and why he allowed this to happen to me. I lived a relatively healthy lifestyle. I had no family history of this or anything similar, and I tried my best to live a holy life. So why me? It was as though I heard the Lord speak to me and say, "In order for to you know that I am a healer and know me in the area of healing, you must know for yourself that I am a healer."

At the time of writing this book, I am believing in God for my healing. First Peter 2:24 (AB) says, "He personally bore our sins in His [own] body on the tree [as on an altar and offered Himself on it], that we might die (cease to exist) to sin and live to righteousness. By His wounds you have been healed."

I'm just waiting on the manifestation of my healing. Psalm 34:19 (KJV) says, "Many are the afflictions of the righteous: but the LORD delivereth him out of them all."

# CHAPTER 3

## Get That Monkey Off Your Back

We all carry a monkey on our back called "our past." We can't move forward, because we're holding on to how it used to be or "I remember when they/you …" We all must let go of our past in order to move forward into our future. I preached a sermon entitled "God Is in Your Future, Waiting On You to Catch Up."

Paul said it best in Philippians 3:13–14 (AB),

> I do not consider, brethren, that I have captured and made it my own [yet]; but one thing I do [it is my one aspiration]: forgetting what lies behind and straining forward to what lies ahead, I press on toward the goal to win the [supreme and heavenly] prize to which God in Christ Jesus is calling us upward.

We must pick up the pieces and leave the past behind us. My wife preached a sermon one time entitled, "Out with the Old and In with the New." You won't get to the new until you get rid of the old. Frustrating, isn't it? God is not holding us back. Now, if God is not holding us back, who or what is? Hmm!

I'll tell you this. Jeremiah 29:11 (AB) says, "For I know the thoughts and plans that I have for you, says the Lord, thoughts and plans for welfare and peace and not for evil, to give you hope in your final outcome." God's plans are not to hurt or harm us. They are to prosper and develop us, along with build our character and integrity. Unlike man, God has our best interest at heart.

All of us have had events, adversities, challenges, and circumstances that left us wounded, hurt, bruised, and scared. Life itself has left many of us bruised, traumatized, and scared. Lord knows we have the battle scars to prove it. Let me be honest right through here. Many of us were hurt in the church. I guess we can say like Zechariah 13:6 (AB) states, "And one shall say to him, what are these wounds on your breast or between your hands? Then he will answer those with which I was wounded [when disciplined] in the house of my [loving] friends."

Sometimes we don't understand God's plans. We think God is doing us an injustice when our enemies attack and attach themselves. How else will you identify your enemies and haters if they don't display their hand? Change your perspective and outlook on the frustration.

There were times when I was facing my own frustrating situations. Others still called upon me to minister to them. I didn't understand how I could minister and still go through it. I learned a lesson really quickly, the difference between a job and ministry. A job stops at a certain time; ministry continues no matter who, what, where, or when. I was once called to the hospital to pray for an individual on his death bed. A person told me, "You need to be careful because I could end up in the same condition."

Needless to say, I was upset. My righteous indignation rose. See, beloved, as hurtful as that was to me, I could not allow or accept the negativity spoken to me in my life. The frustrating aspect of this whole situation was how something so innocent; yet so needed and meaningful to someone on his death bed, could be turned into a hellish situation.

Well, I guess I can say that experience toughened my skin and developed my character. I'm still alive to declare his glory. I'm anointed to preach the gospel and write this book. Paul wrote the sentiments of my heart when he said, "I press toward the mark of the high calling in Christ Jesus."

Another monkey is called "unforgiveness." Child of God, if we are going to move forward to our purpose and destiny, we must forgive others as well as ourselves. We must let go of resentment, grudges, and bitterness. Many of us are holding grudges against those who harmed us sexually, physically, emotionally, mentally, verbally, spiritually, and financially. We think people are plotting against us as well as talking about us. The very people we think are doing these things have actually moved on with their lives, and so should you!

You may say, "I can forgive, but I can't forget!" Absolutely there are things that have happened to us that we will never forget. When I was about five years of age, I was molested. In the sixties, molestation was not something that was discussed among the male gender. It wasn't until way later in life that I came to the realization of what actually happened to me.

One day, someone asked me, "If you saw that person today, would you speak to that individual?"

I replied yes! The love of God in me is greater than the tragedy that happened to me. That doesn't mean we would have lunch, but I would treat this person as the Word instructs. I haven't forgotten the incident, but neither am I holding on to the tragedy, allowing it to hold me back. First Peter 4:8 (AB) says, "Above all things, have intense and unfailing love for one another, for love covers a multitude of sins [forgives and disregards the offenses of others]." I'm not allowing my past to keep me from my destiny. Holding on to the past gives individuals, events, and so on power over you. How frustrating is that?

You must take charge of your life by taking back what the adversary has stolen from you. Say to the adversary, "There's a new sheriff in town." Be like David when he returned from Ziglag. He inquired of the Lord if he should pursue his enemies, and the Lord said, "Pursue and you shall recover all."

Take back your dignity, self-esteem, integrity, character, social status, courage, spirituality, marriage, family, self-worth, effectiveness, sanity, finances, calling, peace, joy, and happiness. Luke 10:19 (AB) reads, "Behold! I have given you **authority** and **power** to **trample** upon serpents and scorpions, and [physical and mental strength and ability] over all the power that the enemy [possesses]; and nothing shall in any way harm you." You have a right to be happy!

Oh yes, beloved, I've experienced church hurt. There were many times I felt like leaving the church. At times, I got so wrapped up in my feelings and what was happening to me that I found it difficult to praise God. Do you know that's what the adversary wanted? He wanted me to lose my momentum. He will use whoever and whatever device he can to keep you from praising God. Frustration will cause you to pray amiss.

I was praying one day and asking God to allow me to backslide. Once again, when you're a person of destiny and purpose, you must be processed, for example, like gold tried in the fire. I once looked to man for answers and solutions.

One day while visiting my mother, she called me into her room, sat me down, and said to me, "You must get to know God for yourself. Establish a relationship with him for yourself."

As a praying woman, mother must have felt what I was going through, or the Lord told her. At this time, I began to pray and ask God to help me to know him for myself. I had to see Jesus for myself. Although I received many prayers from bishops, pastors, and ministers, I still had to look to Jesus for myself. God began to do it for me! I started to feel so much better!

You see, beloved, I had to change my focus from the creature to the creator. Hebrew 12:2 (KJV) says, "Looking unto Jesus the author and finisher of our faith; who for the joy that was set before Him endured the cross despising the shame, and is set down at the right hand of the throne of God."

My family and friends would joke with me and tell me, "Edward, you are not going anywhere. All you know is God. You wouldn't even fit in the world."

During this series, I ministered the same word to the people of God. I told them that they had to get to know God and establish a relationship with him for themselves. Although our leaders play a critical role in our spiritual walk with the Lord as it relates to our development, if they go crazy or walk away from Christendom, we must be rooted and grounded in the Lord by which we will still be able to stand and go forward. So many have allowed themselves to get so wrapped up in leadership that, when the leadership gets frustrated or discouraged or throws in the towel and walks away, it can be challenging to remain standing and not give up.

Oh my! We can't forget about that monkey called confrontation. Many of us are too confrontational, and several of us are not confrontational enough. We must learn to pick our battles. Kenny Rogers once sang, "You've got to know when to hold 'em and know when to fold 'em."

We love to give people a piece of our mind. I believe, if we continue to do so, we won't have much of a mind left. Solomon told us in Ecclesiastes 5:3 (KJV), "A **fool**'s voice is known by multitude of words." There's an old cliché' my mother would often say, "To change a fool against his will is of the same opinion still." In other words, there's no profit or gain in arguing with a fool.

Don't get me wrong. You don't just let people run over you. When I came up in holiness, they taught us that you didn't say anything. You just carried it to the Lord. But I believe God wants us to handle some things on our own. Matthew 5:24 KJV says "Leave there thy gift before the altar, and go thy way; first be reconciled to thy brother, and then come and offer thy gift." First make peace with your brother, and then come back and present your gift."

How you handle confrontation is vitally important to your character and integrity. You cannot allow anyone to change your attitude because of where you're going. Remember I stated earlier that you are a person of destiny and purpose. The devil will use anything and anyone to get you off course. He will do anything and everything to frustrate your purpose. When you allow people to impact your attitude, you literally give them power over you, and the devil sits back and mocks you, "Uh-huh, you're not as strong as you thought you were." Friend, I speak to you now that you take Exousia over the enemy.

I was falsely accused at a particular time, and all manner of untrue things were said about me. I got all riled up, and I was ready to retaliate. Thank God for the family member who pulled me back and said, "Come on, Edward. Don't do it." I'm quite sure from my actions, you can tell I was upset. This should have been one of those times that I should have picked my battle.

When it comes to confrontation, as my early brother used to say, there are times when you have to defend your city. For example, sometimes you have to confront and other times you have to back up and say to yourself, "How will this impact me?"

When I was appointed to a position, I was met with opposition. Even when the Lord positions for promotion and advancement in the kingdom, but then you are told that you're not called or qualified according to man's standard, frustration can easily creep in. In this situation, I chose to handle this confrontation in love and a way in which my integrity and character would remain intact.

My mind went to Joshua 24:13 (NASB), "I gave you a land on which you had not labored, and cities which you had not built, and you have lived in them; you are eating of vineyards and olive groves which you did not plant."

I didn't stop there. I sought the Lord, and Psalm 37:23 (KJV) came to me, "The steps of a good man are ordered by the LORD: and he delighteth in his way."

My friend, we must realize and accept the fact that, when you come into your destiny and purpose, it also creates the gateway for all your haters to show themselves. Second Chronicles 20:15 (KJV) tells us, "The **battle is not yours**, but God's."

There were times when Jesus handled confrontation. Other times, he perceived what his enemies were trying to do so he didn't give them the time of day. Remember the confrontation where the woman was caught in adultery? As a long story short, Jesus told the crowd that he who was without sin was to cast the first stone. He bent down to write on the ground, and when he arose, the crowd had dispersed.

Jesus asked the woman, "Where are your accusers?"

She replied, "I have none."

Jesus said, "Neither do I accuse you. Go and sin no more."

Why not sometimes take that attitude? The Bible says, "We all have sinned and come short of the glory of God." How many times have we wronged someone or spoke ill of another person? When it comes to us, we forget what we've done to others. Luke 6:41–42 (AB) says,

> Why do you see the speck that is in your brother's **eye** but do not notice or consider the **beam** [of timber] that is in your own **eye**? Or how can you say to your brother, Brother, allow me to take out the speck that is in your **eye**, when you yourself do not see the **beam** that is in your own **eye**? You actor (pretender, hypocrite)! First take the **beam** out of your own **eye**, and then you will see clearly to take out the speck that is in your brother's **eye**.

How often do we pray, asking the Lord to change so-and-so when the Lord is saying, "No, you need to change." I realized that I had to change if I wanted to make it as a believer and if I were to receive what God had for me. No matter what others did or didn't do, I agreed or disagreed with what I saw others do. I had to make up my mind that change started with me.

Let's pray.

Lord, I realize I will have frustrations, but help me to handle them in accordance with your Word and your divine will. I realize that frustrations are part of the process that will ultimately prepare me for my future and get me to my Promised Land. Help me to change those things I can change and accept those things I can't. Those things I can't change, I cast them on you, Lord.

Revelation 21:5 (KJV) says, "I make all things new." I realize that, if you're with me, you are more than the world against me. I understand the enemy's plan/purpose is to kill, steal, and try to destroy me, but by the blood of Jesus Christ, his plans for my life are spoiled. His contract has been stamped null, void, and canceled. He is a defeated foe, and in the end, I win! Thanks be unto God who gives me the victory and causes me to triumph.

# CHAPTER 4

## The Waiting Room

In 1994, my mother underwent a five-hour heart bypass surgery. We (family/friends/saints) had to wait in the designated room, that is, the waiting room. I noticed that many were in the room because others had someone undergoing surgery; however, everyone's waiting time was different. We all face various frustrations that we have to deal with. One of the most common frustrations is the wait time.

James 1:4 (AB) encourages us, "But let patience have her perfect work, that ye may be perfect and entire, wanting nothing." We all may be going through various to similar challenges, and although God has no respect of person, our wait time is different. The Bible gives credence to this one thing, "They that wait on the Lord, He shall renew their strength. They shall mount up on wings as an eagle. They shall run and not be weary, and they shall walk and not faint."

Remember Saul and David. David waited for a while for his deliverance from Saul, who tried numerous times to hunt down and kill David. Can you imagine the frustration David had to deal with? He literally was running for his life. David's entire life was uprooted, but he still had to wait on the Lord and be of good courage. He couldn't follow his will, but he had to follow God's.

Now we must remember that David had some opportunities to kill Saul, but he couldn't. Therefore, he didn't. He spared Saul's life. This lets us know that every opportunity that presents itself is not your window of opportunity. What I've said before bears repeating, "Don't sacrifice your future for the present."

Proverbs 15:22 (AB) says, "Where there is no counsel, purposes are frustrated, but with many counselors they are accomplished." Be careful whom you listen to while in the waiting room. Words are a seed. Listening to the wrong persons can lead you to change your confession and profession. Whenever you are waiting on God to deliver, your reactions are different from the world. Job said, "All my appointed time, I'll wait until my change come." Frustration will bring about change one way or other. It can bring about increase or decrease in your life.

Oh, it's so exciting for the man or woman of God to speak into your life, to reveal what God has in store for you. Many attend revivals, conferences, and so on, looking for a word from the Lord. Don't get me wrong. I look for a prophetic word. Consequently, the best word is from the Word of God.

I remember receiving many prophecies that God was going to give me a special anointing. Boy, was I excited. I fell out under the power of the Holy Ghost, got up, shouted, danced, and praised God. After a while, I began to wonder, *Where is this special anointing?*

> Is that how we do? We get caught up in the moment, and once all the excitement is over, we wonder why the prophecy hasn't come to pass.

It was then I realized and I began to experience tremendous adversities and challenges. Someone forgot to tell me that the anointing wasn't going to come without a price. I'm here to say, "Beloved, the anointing costs. It doesn't come without a price." I admonish you, before you get caught up in the prophecy, be aware it's not going to come without a price and your participation.

Just like David, some of you are running for your life. Don't give up yet. Remember— we must run the race with patience. Ecclesiastes 9:11 (AB) says, "I returned and saw under the sun that the race is not to the swift nor the battle to the strong, neither is bread to the wise nor riches to men of intelligence and understanding nor favor to men of skill; but time and chance happen to them all."

The blessing, deliverance, and freedom will come. You have nothing else to do but stand still and see the salvation of the Lord. The Lord is using you to bring about his glory. While you're waiting, keep looking to the hills from which cometh your help. Do know for sure that your help comes from the Lord. I know waiting is hard. I speak from experience that waiting is the difficult phase of the process.

Frustration will come, but it's what you do while you're going through. Don't become dead men/women walking. That is, for example, don't become overwhelmed, bitter, and mad at the Lord. Jesus said, "I came that you might have life and that (life) more abundantly." Even though you're going through tests and trials, you still have life. Sometimes when dealing with frustration before deliverance, you have to follow the pattern of our Lord and Savior, Jesus Christ. Jesus had to escape and steal away for his life during his hours of agony. Stealing away affords you opportunities to reassess, reevaluate, take a look at the bigger picture, and come back refreshed, rejuvenated, and reenergized so you can attack from a different perspective.

I remember my wife receiving several prophecies as well as word on knowledge that she was surrounded around many children or she was seen with a lot of little ones. Now, can you imagine what we thought?

We were like, "Oh no, we're not having any more children."

You can't have a closed mind when God is revealing his plan for your life. Pray and ask God to reveal what he is saying. While you're in the waiting room, increase your capacity. See God before becoming closed-minded. I'll reveal what God was saying to her later in the book.

# CHAPTER 5

## Don't Settle

In the days and times we're living in, so many challenges and adversities are impacting us—health issues, job loss, foreclosures, leaders walking away from ministries, divorce amongst pastors, and so on. So many people are being attacked in their health, like cancer, diabetes, arthritis, aneurisms, and strokes, just to name a few.

If you were like me, you don't have any idea you have it or something has occurred in your body until you go to the doctor. I often say, "You can go to bed in perfect health and wake up the next day and find yourself being challenged in your health." Beloveds, it's not a sin or saint issue. This epidemic is affecting the entire world.

In 2 Kings 7:1 (AB), Elisha gives the king hope of their conditions improving in twenty-four hours. But what do you do when the Word of God has been spoken over your life, and the promise of God doesn't match your present circumstances, or you come through one thing and then suddenly here comes something else? I've been there! How about you come up with a plan to pay off some debt due to receiving extra revenue; however, before you can even put the plan in motion, things begin to happen. What's that cliché? "If it ain't one thing, it's another."

We must remember that God orchestrates our lives. Sometimes God doesn't deliver us out of a thing, but he'll give us the strength to endure or allow that thing to be a thorn in our side to keep us at the altar and keep us humble as well as in his presence. While you're dealing with one thing, here comes another challenge.

After being installed to pastor at Wonder Working Word Church on September 27, 2014, I was excited and happy to see the hand of God and what he spoke over my life manifested. Little did I know, in January 2016, I would be diagnosed with ketoacidosis, which was medically induced due to medication to treat my sarcoidosis. First of all, I would have never thought I would be diagnosed with such a dangerous and deadly disease. My dad and aunts died as result of diabetes, which brought about other health complications.

After the doctor in urgent care told me to go straight to the hospital, my glucose level was five hundred-plus, the highest their equipment could gauge. When I arrived at the hospital and they ran the appropriate test, my glucose level was eight hundred-plus, as high as their equipment could measure. I was hospitalized for a week, a majority of the time in ICU.

I laid in ICU and cried (more than once), asking the Lord, "Why?" With almost everyone I talked to while in the hospital, tears would just begin to flow. It was like I had no control. I would just begin to boo-hoo. Lord, why did you allow this to happen to me after you called me to such an important call and charge? I was just installed, and I reached my destiny, I believed. How could I effectively lead and shepherd your people with this disease that has altered my life?

The Word encourages us that all things work together for the good of them that love the Lord and are the called according to his purpose. Although frustrated, the good caused me to change my eating habits. Not that I was a big sweet eater, but some dietary changes were needed. Beloved, our bodies have to be praise-conditioned. We are vessels of the living God; therefore, we must be in condition for what God wants to do in us, through us, and for us.

> Let me stop right here and thank my church and my ministry of helps for their prayers, support, and watching out for me. Kingdom blessings!

Second Kings 7:3–8 (AB) says,

Now four men who were lepers were at the entrance of the [city's] gate; and they said to one another, "Why should we sit here until we die? If we say, 'We will enter the city' then the famine is in the city and we will die there, and if we sit still here, we will also die. So now come, let us go over to the camp of the Arameans (Syrians). If they let us live, we live; and if they kill us, we will only die." So they got up at twilight to go the Aramean camp. But when they came to the edge of the camp, there was no one there. For the Lord had caused the Aramean army to hear the sound of chariots, and the sound of horses, the sound of a great army. They had said to one another, "The king of Israel has hired against us the kings of the Hittites, and the kings of the Egyptians, to come [and fight] against us."

My wife, Lady Dorothy Butler, said one time in her teachings that sometimes you must take a step back, withdraw yourself, regroup, reassess, and come back stronger.

Reassess your current position and state. Don't let it frustrate you. Sometimes all you need is a push in the right direction or someone to come up with a plan, thought, or motivation to say, "Hey, we might as well do something. If we fail or die, at least we failed or died in action."

Let's look at the four men condition. They were lepers (with an incurable disease). They were exiled. They were social outcasts. Their bodies were infected, and they were impoverished. Have you ever been in a place where one thing had a rippling event (frustrating)?

Look at 2 Kings 7:2 (AB). You can settle by not hearing and believing the Word of God. Disbelief and doubt displeases as well as dishonors God. You're literally saying, "God cannot accomplish what he said. His Word is null and void."

Doubt and disbelief, your current status and situations doesn't align with what God promised, will cause you to see the blessings/deliverance but not take possession. God made a promise to the children of Israel that he would deliver them (and he did) and bring them to that land that flowed with milk and honey.

The spies were sent to spy on the land. They returned with the report that the land was as God said, but there were giants. "Consequently, we are not able to take the city."

Now, first of all, this was frustrating for their pastor (Moses) after deliverance from Egypt. Second, this displeased God because they went by what they saw instead of what God said.

> Sometimes God will allow events and developments to occur so the leader will see what he or she is working with.

Because of their report, they did not take possession of the promise. Whose report will you believe?

We can't lose sight or forget what God has said because of the fortified walls and giants. Strive to be like Caleb or what I call the Caleb generation. Caleb had another spirit. He saw through the eyes of God and the eyes of faith. He said, "Let's go up at once. We're well able."

Jeremiah 17:7 (AB) says, "Blessed [with spiritual security] is the man who believes in and relies on the Lord and whose hope and confident expectation is the Lord."

Expectation is a model of hope, anticipation, belief, and prospect. Don't settle in, could of, should of, and would of. These are frustrating places and thoughts that are designed to prevent us from moving forward. As long as you settle in your current frustrating state, you'll never see your way out. Consequently, you won't take action.

The Word of God denotes to us in Job 5:19 (AB), "He will rescue you in six troubles; in seven nothing that is evil [for you] will touch you." I like the Message Bible. It says, "From one disaster after another He delivers you; no matter what the calamity, the evil can't touch you." I remember receiving letters from the IRS by which they informed my wife and I that we had been randomly selected. And as a result, we were audited. We were randomly selected four different times within the same year (for current and previous tax years), both federal and state.

> We have our taxes prepared professionally.

Randomly selected? Audited four different times by both levels of the government? Whoever heard of such a thing. It's the work of the devil!

Their findings, depending on the federal or state, we owed from $250 to over $3,000. Mind you, we had already received refund checks. Therefore, we had to manage our frustration. Frustration unmanaged will violate your testimony. People respond to you by what they see you do, not by what you say.

# CHAPTER 6

## From the Waiting Room to the Delivery Room

### Handling Frustration after Deliverance

John 16:33 (AB) says, "In this world you have tribulations and trials and distress and frustration, but be of good cheer (take courage; be confident, certain, undaunted)! For I have overcome the world. (I have deprived it of power to harm you and have conquered it for you.)"

Frustration is inevitable. Let's ask Joseph. He made it to the palace, but because he wouldn't sleep with Pharaoh's wife, she made a false accusation, which caused him to be imprisoned. Come here, Hannah. She worked in the temple but was barren, that is, serving the Lord but still lacking something in her life. She made a vow that, if the Lord gave her a child, she would give him back to him. Imagine having a child and then having to give up your young one because of a vow you made out of need.

In chapter two, I mentioned at the time of this book that I believed I was healed of sarcoidosis; however, I was waiting on the manifestation of my healing. Well, wouldn't you know it? After completing my annual twenty-one day fast in January

2011, the manifestation of my healing finally occurred. But guess what? I'm glad I got your attention. I'm dealing with the frustration of what my wife calls flare-ups. My sinuses cause my flare-ups. I have moments when I cough, but it's not like it was at the beginning and not as severe. I still believe I'm healed.

Second Corinthians 2:14 (AB) says, "But thanks be to God, Who in Christ always leads us in triumph [as trophies of Christ's victory] and through us spreads and makes evident the fragrance of the knowledge of God everywhere." Let's dissect that word *triumph*, that is, *conquest, victory, accomplishment, success,* and *achievement.* This is what God causes in every place.

Perhaps you have moved from the waiting room to the delivery room. You have experienced a manifestation in your life. You can say with me, "I am the proof of what God is capable of." Beloved, let me tell you. Sometimes when you move to the delivery room, you experience complications. Remember in chapter four, I spoke on the prophecy my wife received about children. Well, the prophecy came to pass. We are foster parents, and many children—all ages, colors, and genders—surround her. They've come from all backgrounds, including those who were attracted to the same sex and those who were questioning their sexuality. See, I know some of you probably are saying, "I wouldn't have the child in my home."

Question: How will they come to know Christ unless we tell them? We had frustrations from children/teenagers who suffered severe trauma and, as a result, were bed wetters to marijuana smokers, the sexually active, or those who just were the baby's daddy. You see, my friends, we can't pick out of what part of the prophecy we're going to participate in.

I remember watching a television program in the Bahamas. There was a woman in the delivery room having a baby; consequently, the baby was born without complications. However, the mother experienced complications after the baby's birth. She began to immediately hemorrhage. She received blood transfusions to prevent her from bleeding out.

I said that to say this, "After the manifestation of her giving birth to what was inside her, the battle was still on."

After the manifestation of my healing, at times I experience flare-ups, not to mention my doctor sent me to see another specialist, a gasteronical doctor.

After having an esophagus bioscopy, I was diagnosed with geriatrics esophagus reflux disease (GERDS). Beloved, you may be in the delivery room, and manifestation is inevitable, but sometimes you may experience complications. Sometimes the complication is to move you forward or to fortify you for what was just manifested or to further develop.

Now that God has delivered, I've had to go through the reprogramming phase (forgetting, forgiving, and letting go), so I could embrace the glory of the Lord. Do you not know many people can't embrace the glory of the Lord because they haven't learned how to forgive as well as let go?

Question: how do you undo something that you experienced for seven and a half years? As a result of my deliverance, I had to deal with the frustration of becoming accustomed to new methodologies, concepts, and ideals. At times I found myself continuing to do unnecessary things to protect myself as well as making decisions based on what I previously experienced. I had to take a personal interest in my path as well as come to grips with a revolution about what had taken place and what was once was no more.

Deliverance requires knowledge and our participation. We must maintain a Bible-reading, prayer, and fasting life. Our minds must be continually renewed. Deliverance doesn't mean the frustration has gone away. It just means God has delivered, and now there's a new frustration to deal with and fresh challenges to face. Matthew 12:43–45 (NET) says,

> When an unclean spirit goes out of a person, it passes through waterless places looking for rest but does not find it. Then he saith, I will return into my house from whence I came out; and when he is come, he findeth it empty, swept, and garnished. Then goeth he, and taketh with himself seven other spirits more wicked than himself, and they enter in and dwell there: and the last state of that man is worse than the first. Even so shall it be also unto this wicked generation.

Can you imagine after Abraham received the fulfillment of God's promise by Ishmael and Isaac being born that Abraham had to deal with issues of having an illegitimate and legitimate son? Who was going to be his heir? A jealous wife at first told him to go to Hagar and have relations with her. Now Abraham had to contend with a wife whom he has a legitimate son with and a bondswoman (a slave) with whom he had an illegitimate son. As I previously mentioned, Sarah was now jealous. She wanted to ensure her son was the true heir and his father was spending enough time with her son. Now Sarah came to him and told him that Hagar and Ishmael, who was fourteen, had to go. Lord, how do I tell the mother of my firstborn as well as my fourteen-year-old son that they have to go?

Now Hagar had to deal with frustration of being put out, homeless, and not knowing where they were going to go. There weren't any shelters, and they had no relatives. She was thinking, *I didn't ask for this.* Beloved, we must remember that, in the midst of frustration, God will intervene. Genesis 16:10 says, "And the angel of the LORD said unto her, I will multiply thy seed exceedingly, that it shall not be numbered for multitude."

Abraham had to deal with wondering where the mother of his son and his son were? Was he safe? What did he look like? What was he involved in, and what had he evolved into? One thing stuck with me in this story. God appeared to Hagar and made the same promise to her that he made to Abraham. He would make him a great nation. He would multiply him as the stars in the sky.

A common frustration is people—or should I say "your haters"—when they say, "You think you're so much." Or if you were like me, my haters said, "You should have been gone too." Or how about you have to supervise some of the same people who were plotting to get rid of you? It is up to me to let the love of God be shared abroad to others through me. An old cliché my mother would say was, "Kill 'em with kindness."

I began to bask in the thoughts of no more waking up in the middle of the night in cold sweats, being full of fear, anxiety, stress, and worry. Can you imagine the feeling of "no more; it's all over"? It is God who causes us to triumph! Jeremiah 18:6 (AB) says, "Look carefully, as the clay is in the potter's hand, so are you in My hand." We will forever be in the potter's hand. The scripture gives credence, "O house of Israel, cannot I do with you as this potter? Saith the Lord; Behold as the clay is in the potter's hand, so are you in mine hand."

I had to bring my will in line with God's, that is, be submissive to God's will. Bringing my will in line with God's is the best move I made. It's better to bow now rather than later. You must spend time with God in prayer and fasting.

The Lord gets upset with us when he tells us we can have something and we say we can't like the children of Israel. Moses sent out the spies, and when they returned, they reported that the land was like it was told to them, but because of the giants, they would not be able to possess the land. Here's the leader, for example, pastor, who has God's Word, but the saints who have walked, talked, and saw God's miraculous power came back with a report of defeat instead of victory. Joshua and Caleb came back with the same report, but instead of speaking out of defeat and what they saw, Caleb reported we were well able. Second Corinthians

5:7 (AB) says, "For we walk by faith (we regulate our lives and conduct ourselves by our conviction or belief respecting men's relationship to God and divine things, with trust and holy fervor; thus we walk) not by sight or appearance."

Beloved, our lives must be regulated by our beliefs and convictions, despite what it looks like. If God said it, that settles it. I had to learn that oftentimes when God gives you a word or tells you what he's going to do, the present condition and circumstances will not and does not always line up with what God has spoken to you. We must develop an Abrahamic attitude, "Abraham staggered not at the promises of God." Confess right. (I'm blessed because I believe like Abraham).

Upon moving from the waiting room to the delivery room, you can experience what I call lag time, which is a wait. It is out of your control. I remember my son and daughter applied for jobs, had their interviews, and were hired, but they couldn't start working right away. Upon accepting the job, unknown to them, the companies required additional documents that had to be mailed to them from other sources. It was not something they would have or carry around on a normal day. This is quite frustrating, especially when you've been hired and want to start working. If you allow the enemy to fight in your mind, you will begin to display signs of frustration. Notice, they weren't told they didn't have the jobs. Just additional personal information was needed. They were at the mercy of others. Thank the Lord that the wait wasn't that long!

The Lord blessed us to build a church. We moved from the waiting room to the delivery room. However, we met with unforeseen frustration. Some of our strong and consistent tithers went home to be with Jesus. What am I saying? Revenue was lost. Frustration was increased, ensuring all bills were to be paid. Some key as well as some of (what we would classify) prominent members physically left the ministry. There went vacancies and expertise we once had and were now gone. Frustration increased. The remaining members were wearing many hats. Now we must intensify our soul-winning efforts to ensure souls were added to the ministry, and last but not least, don't let people become territorial. For example, the present body doesn't become closed-minded to new ideas and concepts and remains open to a fresh approach to new blood that the Lord will bring in.

Early one August morning, I was praying, pouring out my heart to the Lord about the ministry and its status. One thing I said to him, "You blessed us to build this church. Why are we going continually around this mountain? How long are we going to be in this wilderness? I know you didn't bring us and allow us to build this church for us to fail." The Lord revealed to me that I was to "strengthen that which remains."

He took me to Revelation 3:2 (AB), "Rouse yourselves and keep awake, and strengthen and invigorate what remains and is on the point of dying." I stopped praying to look up some of the words so I would understand my assignment. Strengthen meant to set fast, to turn resolutely in a certain direction or confirm, to fix, or to establish and steadfastly set. I then understood my assignment. The people of God needed to know that, through these times of uncertainty and frustration, God was still with us. He hadn't left us. We had depended, trusted, and relied on him. His plan was not to destroy us, but he was thinking good thoughts of us, and he was going to give us an expected end. Things were going to change. God was going to move in his time and season. The leadership had to remain encouraged and motivated.

# CHAPTER 7

# R U Ready for the Blessing?

P art of handling frustration after the blessing is receiving the proper instructions prior to the blessing. The Bible denotes to us, "We (people) perish e.g., are destroyed due to the lack of knowledge." Many of us have received and continue to receive prophesies. As a matter of fact, many people go to revivals, conferences, and so on, looking for a word from the Lord. Oh, it's so exciting for someone to speak into your life and/or reveal what God was getting ready to do. I remember receiving many prophecies that God was going to give me a special anointing. Boy, I was so excited. I shouted and praised God. After a while, I begin to wonder, *Where is this special anointing?*

This bears repeating: I failed to realize that I began to experience tremendous adversities and challenges. Although I received prophecies regarding a special anointing, no one ever told me that anointing doesn't come without a cost. Beloved, the anointing costs! I admonish you, before you get caught up in the prophecy, be aware that it's not going to come without a price and your participation. You must spend time with God in prayer and fasting.

Align your finances with the Word of God, tithing/managing your finances. My brothers and my sisters, practicing the world's economic system will not activate the promises of God in our lives. When we practice God's economic system, this is when the promises of God are activated in our lives. Tithing and managing your finances is all part of the process of handling frustration. The Word of God gives us to know that, if we don't pay our tithes, we are cursed with a curse. Beloved, we're obligated to honor God as he has blessed us. He will also bless us to be a blessing. The fulfillment of God's promises in our lives is predicated on our ability to come into compliance with his Word. If you be faithful over a few things, I'll make you a ruler over many. Isaiah 1:19 (AB) says, "If you are willing and obedient." No matter what frustrations we're facing, obedience to God will be coping mechanisms that will see us through the frustrations of life. Obedience will cause blessings to come upon us and overtake us. Blessings will literally chase us down.

There are those who are teaching that tithing is not biblical, but according to what I've read as well as been taught and seen work, it's biblical. I've come too far to change now, to doubt and question God's financial system. I often say, "If tithing is wrong, then I don't want to be right." Adam met a frustrating situation after God pronounced blessings, dominion, and multiplication on his life. He gave Adam specific instruction: don't touch the tree in the midst of the garden for it belongs to him.

But Adam was deceived; therefore, his situation became frustrating. He and his wife were punished. He and all the male gender would earn their living by the sweat of their brow. Our women would bring forth children in pain. The ground and so forth was cursed. See, beloved, you can be frustrated after the blessings if we fail to align ourselves with the Word of God. Maintain consistency, remain committed, and demonstrate loyalty to the Almighty God. The tree in the midst of the garden was tithed unto God. It was holy unto God; it belonged to God. Don't touch that which belongs to God. Tithes are holy unto God. It belongs to God. Proverbs 14:12 (KJV) says, "There is a way which seemeth right unto a man, but the end thereof are the ways of death." It bears repeating in Proverbs 16:25 (KJV), a serious matter!

We must understand that we can't circumvent (find a way around) God's will for our lives. We must not let challenges and adversities frustrate us. God uses challenges and adversities before the blessings as part of the process to prepare for our blessings and promises as well as challenges and adversities after the blessing and fulfillment of the promises to prepare us for the next phase of glory in our lives.

Let's look at Moses. After the fulfillment of one promise, Moses and the children of Israel faced another challenge. When Pharaoh let the children of Israel go, God hardened Pharaoh's heart. He and his army pursued the children of Israel. Can you imagine the very thing God delivered you from is now pursuing you? After he became second-in-command in Egypt, Joseph was pursued by Potipher's wife. She attempted to seduce and lie on him, and as a result, he was imprisoned.

Paul met with challenges and adversities after each victory. He and Silas was imprisoned, but instead of getting frustrated, Paul understood the suffering of the present couldn't compare to the glory that was to be revealed. The suffering he was enduring was only temporal. My friend, that frustration is only temporary. When Paul was shipwrecked, God promised that no one would be lost. And no one was. I preached a message one time, "Wet, Impacted, but Not Affected."

I want to reiterate that frustration doesn't go away, but we can let it impact us negatively. Everyone on the journey was saved; however, when they made it to shore, a viper (a snake) bit Paul, but Paul shook the viper off into the fire. His hand was whole. The enemy expected his hand to swell up and for him to die, but no harm came to him. When frustration comes, shake it off in the fire. That is, take time to regroup, reassess, and keep it moving. Your enemy is expecting you to die.

When he walked on the earth, Jesus was led by his goal and objective, to redeem and reconcile us back to the Father. He was constantly challenged and met with adversities via the Scribes, Pharisees, and unbelievers. He even was met with a challenge on the cross from the thief on his left side. The thief said, "If you be God, come down, and save yourself and us too!"

But for the greater glory, he stayed on the cross instead of letting frustration overcome him. When the thief on his right side asked Jesus to forgive him and remember him when went to his Father, Jesus stopped dying long enough to say, "This day shall thy be with me in paradise."

Come on, beloved. Let's pull up our bootstraps and recognize challenges, adversities, chaos, and havoc is part of the process, not to frustrate us. Matthew 13:26 (NET) says, "When the plants sprouted and bore grain, then the weeds also appeared." When we began to experience our deliverance (the tares), frustration will appear. And it's without your permission and/or approval.

Understand, beloveds, just because God delivers you from homosexuality/ lesbianism, gambling (including going to the boat), not tithing, manipulation, and so on, this doesn't mean temptation won't rear its ugly head. Just because you were delivered from lying doesn't mean temptation isn't going to happen. Just because you put a stop to that relationship you've been in and God delivers you from all the feelings, emotion, hurt, and pain, this doesn't mean the other person is not going to try to entangle you or stop pursuing you, keeping you in his or her control. I know I said this in the previous chapter, but as it's often said, repetition is the mother of learning. Luke 11:24–26 (NET) says,

> When an unclean spirit goes out of a person, it passes through waterless places looking for rest but not finding any. Then it says, "I will return to the home I left. When it returns, it finds the house swept clean and put in order. Then it goes and brings seven other spirits more evil than itself, and they go in and live there, so the last state of that person is worse than the first." So, we see the enemy doesn't go away, he comes back with reinforcement and tenacity.

First Timothy 6:12 (AB) says, "Fight the good fight of the faith; lay hold of the eternal life to which you were summoned and [for which] you confessed the good confession [of faith] before many witnesses." We must fight to maintain our deliverance and not with carnal weapons because the weapons of our warfare are not carnal, for example, human weapons, but made powerful through God to the pulling-down strongholds, for instance, frustration, manipulation, and intimidation.

Surround yourself with like-minded people. Iron sharpens iron. Proverbs 13:20 (AB) says, "He who walks [as a companion] with wise men will be wise." Are we truly ready for the life-changing blessing? I often say there's a blessing or opportunity that can revolutionize your life.

One day, I was watching the news, and a past lottery winner was being interviewed. This individual stated that he wished he had never won because of all the aftermath that was still occurring. Now you and I would probably say that the person was crazy, but we don't know the frustration he faced since becoming wealthy. Consider the constant solicitations or lack of peace or privacy. Also think about estranged family showing up and or calling or maybe individuals who have already been helped financially aren't satisfied or have mismanaged their finances. They will continue calling asking and even begging. Perhaps these same families, after being refused, are talking about him and so on. This would be the perfect opportunity to seek advice. Proverbs 11:14 (KJV) says, "Where no counsel is, the people fall: but in the multitude of counsellors there is safety." Our purposes are being disappointed when we don't seek advice. Our plans are upset and frustrated when there's no guidance.

Jeremiah 23:4 (AB) says, "I will set up shepherds over them who will feed them. And they will not be afraid any longer, nor be terrified, nor will any be missing." Keep in mind that pastors, church leaders, mentors, and coaches are in place to supplement the guidance of the Holy Spirit, not the other way around. We must let God be our primary teacher and mock the perfect man.

Our bodies are to be conditioned to handle our praise. We often say, "I got a praise, and I got to get it out" when our bodies aren't conditioned to get the praise out. Often we can't shout and dance for the Lord because our bodies are out of condition because we've dealt with our frustration in a negative way. There are unnecessary weights that need to be stripped off, sins that need to be laid aside, or a combo of both. Our bodies are the temple of the Holy Ghost; therefore, if our bodies house the Holy Spirit, it must be in the proper condition. To avoid frustration in our health, adjust your dietary intake, and adhere to your preventive health care plan. If you haven't had a physical, go get checked out. Praise demands response. Consequently our bodies react to praise.

David's body was conditioned to handle his praise. When he saw the ark of the covenant coming from Obededom's house, he asked for his ephod and danced before the Lord. The presence of the Lord will outdo any frustrating situation. Miriam grabbed the tambourine and began to dance before the Lord when the children of Israel crossed the Red Sea.

According to Psalms, praise is comely. For example, it is order, it is necessary, and it is appropriate. We are to clap our hand, make a joyful noise unto the Lord, sing a new song, give him the fruit of our lips continually, and dance before the Lord. The word *God* even addresses bodily exercise. Timothy said bodily exercise is good and has some value; however, it won't give us eternal life. We must balance bodily exercise and spiritual exercise (spiritual training).

Get your dance back!

# CHAPTER 8

## Frustration Deteriorates

**L**et go of frustration. I preached a message entitled, "Hoarder, Let It Go." Maybe you say I can't let things go because I've become a hoarder and I can't let go. Hoarding is a psychological problem that impacts the mind. You have become toxic, bitter, unforgiving, angry, unorganized, secluded, alienated, and swallowed up by the things we refused to let go. Some can't even see that you're holding on to the past. Because it doesn't mix, we have been overtaken, and our very lives have been consumed. Some of us are literally out of control. There's no discipline. We end up buried alive.

We must let go of what happened in our childhood, take what happened to us, turn it into triumph, take the defeat, and turn it into victory. I must focus on my aftercare therapy and be ye transformed by the renewing of my mind, for example, redirect my mind, thoughts, and even outlook.

My wife preached a powerful message one time entitled "Out with Old, In with the New." Let go of the frustration of wanting to get even and seek revenge. Let go of bitterness and unforgiveness.

**Avoid procrastination.** Allow me to be transparent. Procrastination is an area of focus for me. I'm quite sure we all remember the old cliché, "Don't put off tomorrow what you can do today." The very thing we're procrastinating about is the very thing that will catapult us into our destiny or the very idea, concept, and business opportunity that will bring about God's grace in our lives. Procrastination sets in when our minds are filled with what-if thoughts of failure, fear, doubt, and incompetence that infiltrate our minds or when we try to see the outcome before we even begin. We want that safety net!

**Frustration about.** Many of us have a "what about syndrome." I allowed the "ation" family: frustration, procrastination, hesitation, to constrict me like a python. An old song says, "I don't worry about tomorrow. I just live from day to day. I don't borrow from its sunshine, for the skies may turn to grey. I don't worry about the future, for I know what Jesus said, and today he walks beside me for he knows what lies ahead."

I know many of us are fearful to leave our comfort zone. We would be overjoyed if God allowed us to look into tomorrow. There would be no question of direction, decision, or outcome. Boy, the fear of the unknown would be eradicated. I remember during my career after being promoted that frustration reared its ugly head. I had to make a life- and career-altering decision. Boy, I was all over the place, both mentally and emotionally. I agonized and pondered. I sought advice instead of doing what I knew to do best.

Finally I prayed to my heavenly Father but didn't get an answer. I remember what I told the Lord during the time I was unemployed, "I would never quit another job." I recalled the lesson that I learned when I walked off a previous job. I made my decision based on previous life's lessons, and everything worked out in my favor. Today, my career and life is intact. Talking about frustration after deliverance? The outcome was a win-win for everyone!

If God allows us the privilege or luxury to look into or view the future, we would become arrogant and self-sufficient. We would not seek his guidance and trust. We would not trust, that is, rely on him. We would trust in our own ability.

Peter said it this way, "Casting all your cares (all your anxieties, all your worries, and all your concerns, once and for all) on Him, for He cares about you (with deepest affection, and watches over you very carefully)" (1 Peter 5:7 AB).

We must not compare ourselves to others. Be yourself. Say to yourself, "I will confess and praise You for You are fearful and wonderful and for the awful wonder of my birth! Wonderful are Your works, and that my inner self knows right well" (Ps. 139:14 AB). While we're in a state of procrastination, opportunities are passing us by.

Procrastination sets in when we think too much. We begin to lean to our own understanding. While writing this book, I stopped and asked myself, "Why do this? Everyone has written a book. If I'm going to reach my destiny, it can be done through other means." But for some reason, completing this book would not leave me. I continued to hear, "Write the book." My wife often asked me, "Where are you with your book? Are you finished?" As I knew that others reached their destiny or headed into their destiny, a sense of urgency overwhelmed me to complete what God told me to do, this feeling of not obeying God would come over me. I would break out in sweats, and my heart would race. I could feel my heartbeat in my head. Consequently butterflies would begin to flood my stomach. I felt like I was in my childhood when I knew I was in trouble. I'm late, y'all, but you know what? I had to gain a mind-set, set a plan of execution, and then execute. It's not too late!

If you be faithful over a few things, I'll make you a ruler of many. Pray with participation. God is not going to do everything. He'll work along with us. Matthew 7:6 (AB) says, "Do not give that which is holy (the sacred thing) to the dogs, and do not throw your pearls before hogs, lest they trample upon them with their feet and turn and tear you in pieces."

Proverbs 13:20 (KJV) says, "He that walketh with wise men shall be wise: but a companion of fools shall be destroyed." I had to bring my will in line with God's, that is, be submissive to his will. Bringing my will in line with God's is the best move I made. It's better to bow now than later.

A man will escape the anxieties (frustrations) of Proverbs 6:3–5 (AB) if he avoids fellowship with those who often desire financial assistance. He who hates suretyship (cosigning) will be better off than those who allow themselves to be entangled with spurious financial entanglements. Proverbs 22:7 (AB) says, "The borrower is the servant of the lender."

I was taught when I was growing up in the church that we were to owe no man nothing but to love him. If the person hasn't paid you back from the first time, why continue to cast your money to the individual who has yet to pay you back for the first loan? Repeating, Matthew 7:6 (AB) says, "Do not give that which is holy (the sacred thing) to the dogs, and do not throw your pearls before hogs, lest they trample upon them with their feet and turn and tear you in pieces." My momma used to say, "I'm not going to let you continue to hit my head against the wall until it becomes soft like cornbread."

Somewhere you have to rise and be strong and say no! Empower the borrower. Let the borrower know that there is no benefit in going into debt or deeper into debt. Debt causes frustration. Debt not managed can be a permanent solution to what was supposed to be a temporary problem. Take a step back!

**Take God at his word.** Oftentimes when God speaks a word into our lives rather through his vessels or directly to us, our situations and circumstances don't and won't line up with what he's spoken. Number 23:19 (NET) says, "God is not a man, that he should lie, nor a human being, that he should change his mind. Has he said, and will he not do it? Or has he spoken, and will he not make it happen?"

**Don't allow yourself to frustrate.** My brothers and sisters, you can be part of your own as well as someone else's frustration. We as human beings have so many idiosyncrasies, issues, and hang-ups that we ourselves can be frustrating to others. Oftentimes when I have a document that I wrote proofread and have it signed off on, I tend to want to reread, add more content, and so on. And the individuals who have already given their approval have to tell me to, "Send it, Edward." Because I'm a perfectionist, it sometimes is a weakness to others and me. Don't impose your strength or weakness on others.

**Failing to balance.** Whatever it took to handle frustration before the blessings, it's going to take that and more to handle it after the blessing. I remember being appointed pastor of my church. I had to make a conscious decision to maintain balance in my marriage.

I hear of pastors leaving ministries because of spiritual burnout, disgruntled members, discouragement, feelings of underappreciation, and loss of vision. I've heard of pastors falling into sex traps, destroying their families and ministries. We can't allow feelings of frustration and items previously mentioned to ensnare us. As a leader, the standard and the expectation is high because your call came from a higher calling. Therefore, we should be equipped to handle these frustrations. How can you lead or shepherd if you're not willing to fight? Paul had to fight!

First ladies face frustration of feeling underappreciated. They must live with their spouse, seeing and helping them through their frustrations. They face the challenge of keeping the home running like a well-oiled machine. I can speak for my wife. She prays for me in my capacity of husband, father, and pastor. I know she didn't sign on to this when she married me. Who knew? But knowing God's will and what God had for me, she submitted to his will. Of course, she was already serving in the capacity of senior assistant pastor under our former pastor.

We keep God as our focal point. He's the center of our lives, acknowledging him and recognizing his power to keep us. It's not easy all the time. Sometimes the flesh becomes dangerous, but we bring the flesh under subjection. We must keep our assignment and the expectation ever before us. To him, much is given, and much is required!

Don't violate your testimony. Satan has weapons of mass destruction to render us ineffective and ultimately destroy us: carelessness, pride, thinking more highly than we should, spiritual weakness, unforgiveness, and bitterness. Paul said he could preach and be a castaway if he didn't bring his flesh under subjection. Once again, you don't know who's looking and watching you. Don't frustrate others by the life you lead.

# CHAPTER 9

# Frustration about Dress

Matthew 6:28–31 (KJV) encourages us in these words,

> And why take ye thought for raiment? Consider the lilies of the field, how they grow; they toil not, neither do they spin: And yet I say unto you, That even Solomon in all his glory was not arrayed like one of these. Wherefore, if God so clothe the grass of the field, which to day is, and to morrow is cast into the oven, shall he not much more clothe you, O ye of little faith? Therefore take no thought, saying, What shall we eat? or, What shall we drink? or, Wherewithal shall we be clothed?

But there's a condition we must meet. Seek first his righteous kingdom, and all these other things will be added. It is our Father's pleasure to give us the kingdom.

Why are we anxious or become frustrated over what God is responsible for handling? We often worry and frustrate over things that are not in our control. There's an old song we used to sing when I was coming up in the church, and every now and then, we sing it today, "Be not dismayed whatever betides. God will take care of you." There is a lane called faith that we must remain in, no matter the frustration situation.

Beloveds, God is obligated to take care of us. If he's taking care of the birds that fly, the flowers in the fields and in your gardens, and so on, these things can't praise or worship him. If God is doing all of this for nonpraisers or worshippers, what makes you think he won't take care of us and more?

We are to entrust our lives, along with our daily affairs and decisions, to God. He wants to be involved in every aspect of our lives. He will illuminate your path. He will go before you. He sees what we can see. I'll use my wife and I as an example. As foster parents and adoptive parents, we look to God for his guidance. Although a child's background may be off the chain, the Lord will lead us to go ahead and accept the referral and then other occasions, He'll let us know that the placement will not be successful. He does this in many ways. We just have to be open to his voice, direction, and/or what he has disclosed. Psalms 32:8 (AB) says, "I will instruct you and teach you in the way you should go; I will counsel you [who are willing to learn] with My eye upon you."

On July 13, 2013, my pastor, Apostle Aleta McCurty, after preaching an anointed message, called my wife and I and informed Wonder Working Word that I was to pastor the church. She advised them that she was following the leading and obeying God. My prelate installed me as pastor on September 27, 2014. Since that time, I've faced and dealt with many frustrations, yet because I have a charge and calling, I was told I can't run, give up, or walk away from the charge. I've had to deal with the good, the bad, and the ugly. I've had moments where it looked like everything was going the opposite direction of what God had spoken or showed me. All of a sudden, it was as though God was showing me that he was in the midst by what was being accomplished.

I've had frustrating times of not knowing what I should preach, asking God all week, studying, looking into the Word to get a word, and nothing. Frustrating! Then it appears at the eleventh hour. The Lord speaks. What a sigh of relief and joy. I've been dressed!

My desire to be effective in the kingdom is so strong that sometimes it's frustrating and brings tears to my eyes. I want to see Wonder Working Word Church grow both naturally and spiritually. I want see God's people healed, delivered, saved, and set free. I often tell the Lord, "You reach the people where I can't reach them. You go where I can't go and do what I can't do." I've had on many occasions to realize my limitations. I've had to say, "Lord, I can only handle the things that's in my power."

Beloveds, we must control the things we can control. And for those things we can't control, we should place them in the hands of the Lord. Our frustration occurs when we step out of our role. His hands are not too short where he can't handle our situations, challenges, and circumstances.

Being the pastor of the most wonderful congregation of three years has been sometimes frustrating for me because of my desire to see growth. I remembered the book of Acts and how souls were added to the church and the frequency. I prayed to the Lord, "We're doing everything we know to do from media ministry, community outreach, outdoor services, passing out tracts, and personal witnessing, just to name a few."

My journey to pastoralship wasn't an easy one; therefore, I would often allow a spirit of comparison by which I was comparing myself and the ministry to other leaders and ministries. Allowing the spirit of comparison to control your thoughts, sight, and emotions can be the most frustrating, depressing, and spiritually debilitating feeling one can have. I had to fight and gain control of that spirit. I had to focus on what God revealed to me years before I even started pastoring. I have a journal that I wrote what I believed God had revealed to me during my prayer time, when I was asleep, and when I was by myself.

Your journey to your destiny will not be easy. You will meet with all types of frustrations, but you can overcome and gain the victory. On the flip side, you must remain aware and alert because that spirit can resurface. The Bible says (and I'm paraphrasing), "When the enemy sees the house swept and clean, he'll come back stronger and more with reinforcements than original." He wants to regain the territory, but you have to tell him that he's trespassing on private property. Tell him, "And the Lord God rebukes you, and so do I."

Let me speak to our youth right here. You're dealing with the frustration of peer pressure and constricting/restricting environment at home and church. You may have feelings of no one loves you and understands you, along with cyberbullying and cyber sexual harassment, low self-esteem, sexual predators, sexting, as well as "everybody's doing it syndrome."

First, I want to tell you that God loves and cares about you. Don't let no one despise your youth! You are valuable to God, and there is a place in the kingdom for you. God is a God of balance. He's not just for the older generation; he's out for you too! You must gain your own relationship with God. It's not optional. Be more than a survivor, but thrive. Do more than exist. Be a producer. Don't be a conformist; be a transformist. The Word of God encourages us not to conform to the world. Be transformed by the renewing of our mind.

Seek help. Find a confidant, someone you can trust. There are those who can give you advice, instruction, direction, and teaching because they've been where you are trying to go. Allow yourself to become a work in progress (WIP). Remain open to coaching and mentoring. Allow God to cultivate you and your gift.

God knows your name. He's not thinking what you're thinking. Be that force to reckon with.

# CHAPTER 10

## From God's Mouth to Your Ears

There are commonsense principles, concepts, tools, and techniques that are not necessarily faith- or Bible-based.

One thing I've discovered is that people are not going to do for you or go to the extent you would go for them. This is a primary area of frustration that happens before as well as after deliverance. Our expectation of people and what they do and don't do is based on what we do for them. Well, if you don't change that perception, you will be frustrated in everything. I've seen people bend over backward for others, myself included, only to meet with frustration. I've driven two hours to preach, and when it came time for those individuals to reciprocate, it was too far, and they didn't mind voicing it.

So here's a tool or concept you can immediately put into action. Learn to say no. It's not going to send you to hell. It may keep you from hell. Even Jesus said no in Luke 9:54–56 (AB),

> And when His disciples James and John observed this, they said, Lord, do You wish us to command fire to come down from heaven and consume them, even as Elijah did? But He turned and rebuked and severely censured them. He said, you do not know of what sort

of spirit you are, For the Son of Man did not come to destroy men's lives, but to save them [from the penalty of eternal death]. And they journeyed on to another village.

People will use you as long as you allow it.

You may have the available resources at your disposal or may have the answers, but sometimes you have to look at the greater good. Matthew 26:51–54 (AB) says,

> And behold, one of those who were with Jesus reached out his hand and drew his sword and, striking the body servant of the high priest, cut off his ear. Then Jesus said to him, Put your sword back into its place, for all who draw the sword will die by the sword. Do you suppose that I cannot appeal to My Father, and He will immediately provide Me with more than twelve legions [more than 80,000] of angels? But how then would the Scriptures be fulfilled, that it must come about this way?

What will your yes bring about or prevent?

Be mindful of the wear-down syndrome. Like children, they'll plead with you until you give in, they wear you down, or you become so frustrated that, out of your frustration, you give in. Don't just throw up your hands and say yes.

In decision-making, weigh your options even if you're interested. Don't look so eager. Don't let on that you're ready to jump at the first option. I once attended a time-share presentation, and they presented many options after my wife and I said no repeatedly. Had we said yes, we would have left $38,000 in debt. It felt so good to refuse and know that we left our vacation the same way we arrived, with no additional debt.

Let me say here, if there is a partnership or spouse, you must be on the same page. My wife and I discussed our position, and more importantly, we maintained that stance. Now what you must understand about my wife is, in certain situations, when she's adamant, her patience will become very thin. Therefore, I had to make her aware that, although we had taken our position, the presenter was only doing his or her job.

Think through your decision before making it final. People know when they've encountered vulnerability. They will play on your sensitive side or give you a sad sob story. They're going to have all their ducks in a row. They'll have their plan of attack to play on your sensitive side. I've seen in the natural and the spiritual. I've seen money given to false promises and expectations. This has happened even after people have sought out advice and counsel and not merely by one person, but by a multitude. Why ask if you're not going to follow through with the guidance, advice, or counsel you received?

Do your due diligence so you can make informed decisions. We have many research tools, technology, and agencies at our disposal to help us make well-informed decisions. You don't have to rush into it now. That will cause frustration later.

Don't be a yes person. Measure like this. If it's too good to be true, more than likely, it's not. If that's true, then I have some swampland in Alaska for sale.

Don't make hasty, uninformed decisions and then look to God to get you out. Every opportunity is not a window of opportunity. Don't disclose your vision, dream, or project before it's time. As I was writing this book, I became so excited. Especially as I was coming to a close, I wanted to share excerpts and so on with others, but I had to remember that if I share everything now, there would be no reason to get the book. Predisclosure can be a dream/vision killer.

Excitement is positive but can be also frustrating if it's not controlled. Timing is everything in the season of excitement. You see the hand of God and what he's promised being manifested. Hold up. Hold up. Count up the cost. It can put you out there before God's ready to put you on display. Sponsorship comes with benefits. Follow his lead. Let the Lord be your partner. No partnership, no sponsorship, no support, no backing, and no protection. Psalm 37:5 (AB) encourages us to submit our way to God, allowing him to be our guide. Include him in our affairs, even those that seem complicated and perplexing. He wants to be our partner.

Don't let the fear of failure frustrate you. Let me tell you that you will experience failure in life and in Christendom. But don't let that frustrate you. Use that frustration to pull you up out of what you're in, rather if it's life in general or in Christendom. Perhaps you failed or are failing in your walk with Christ. Listen and start speaking over your life. Speak what God has spoken to you. Declare what God has declared to you.

Genesis 1:14 (AB) says, "Then God said, 'Let there be light-bearers (sun, moon, stars) in the expanse of the heavens to separate the day from the night, and let them be useful for signs (tokens) [of God's provident care], and for marking seasons, days, and years.'"

Read Genesis 8:22. Discern and understand your season. The Bible declares, just as the spring, summer, and winter, there's seed time and harvest time. To everything there is a season and a time. If you notice, with each changing season, the climate changes depending on where you are, along with the mood of the people, the atmosphere, and church attendance. People hang out more, leaves change colors, flowers bloom, and specific fruits are available. Animals go in or come out of hiding, shed or grow more hair, and store up food. I can go on. It is the same way in life and Christendom. God has and knows our season. We have to operate in the perimeters of our season. Once you discern and understand the season you're in, it will help you handle the frustration of it all.

I just want to reiterate that, upon your deliverance, you'll face new frustrations. In the church, they say it like this, "New levels, new devils!"

Pull on Jesus Christ, our Lord and Savior!

# CHAPTER 11

·····························································

# In Crisis, Trust God

·····························································

Don't let frustration be a motivation killer. Don't let it kill your momentum. Don't let it stunt your growth. Don't let frustration keep you from advancing in your deliverance.

Accept what God allows and ask him for next steps. We often fight against what God has and hasn't allowed. We don't fight against those things. Don't operate out of artificial intelligence (AI). Operating out of AI simply means your information is fake and false. It's reproduced. When our decisions are based on AI, we frustrate our own purpose and destiny. During crisis, we must seek God, and we shall find him. Seeking God says, "He's my partner. He knows the way I take. His data and intel is current, reliable, infallible, and foolproof, if we follow."

David experiences victory on the battlefield and returns home with his men, only to discover that they've lost everything. All had been taken, including wives and children. The same men that fought with him now turned on him to stone him. Facing discouragement, he encouraged himself. He asked God if he shall pursue and recover all. God said, "Pursue, and you shall recover all." David trusted God in crisis.

As long as we have God's blessings and promise of victory, we'll be victorious in spite of. Keep your momentum. Know your pace as well as limitations. It's not a competition.

God will allow you to frustrate the words of the enemy. When the Lord came down in the fire and no harm came to Shedrach, Meshach, and Abednego, they frustrated the word of Nebuchadnezzar. Nebuchadnezzar had expected one outcome, but God had another.

Joseph faced many frustrations on his journey to his destiny. His siblings hated on him because of a coat. He was thrown in a pit because of a dream. He was rescued and sold into slavery, which landed him in the palace. He was admired and sought after undenounced to him. He was lied on and accused of rape, which landed him in prison. He excelled at whatever he did. The Lord blessed whatever he put his hands to do. While in prison, he interpreted a dream for the butler and the baker, and he was favored while in prison. The Word of God says, "Your gift will make room for you and bring you before great men."

Jehoshaphat was thirty-five when he began to reign, and he reigned for twenty-five years. He was a reformist. He refused to bow and worship Baalim. His conviction was that one couldn't worship idols and God simultaneously. Jehoshaphat trusted God in a crisis. A great multitude had invaded Jehoshaphat. Although he was afraid, he sought to hear from God and receive his guidance. He called a fast and prayer. When you seek the Lord, you shall find him, and he will favor you.

Second Corinthians 4:8–10 (NLT) says,

> We are pressed on every side by troubles, but we are not crushed.
> We are perplexed, but not driven to despair. We are hunted down,
> but never abandoned by God. We get knocked down, but we are not

destroyed. Through suffering, our bodies continue to share in the death of Jesus so that the life of Jesus may also be seen in our bodies.

As you can see, the body must be conditioned.

When I was growing up in the church and we would break out with this song, what we then called "Holy Ghost songs," one in particular comes to mind, "When I think about Jesus and what he's done for me, when I think about Jesus and how he set me free, I can dance, dance, dance, dance all night." We would shout, what we now call dance.

We ought to want to give God our best, and that includes our bodies. He deserves our best. As you can see from 2 Corinthians, we're going to experience one thing after the other, but we're not abandoned. Don't let frustration take your endurance. As believers, we must condition our bodies just as athletes condition theirs.

Don't let frustration bind you up, make you sick, and wear down your body. Remember—God works the night shift. Things often intensify at night. Fever goes higher at night. Pain becomes greater at night and so on. During your night season, God is at work. The enemy uses our night season to frustrate us so it will appear that God is not with us in order to siphon our strength, will, purpose, praise, and dance. Isaiah 40:29 (TLB) says, "He gives power to the tired and worn out, and strength to the weak."

Beloveds, life can be, as a matter of fact, hard. However, God is with us. He allows frustrating, overwhelming situations so we will continually be acquainted with his power. Our trust and reliance will remain in him. We'll stay on our face and in his presence. He will come and strengthen us. He will wipe the sweat from our brow. We can't let frustrating circumstance close the doors of opportunity. Look for another door and move the opportunity to a fair playing field.

My story goes back when my nephew, a son in the gospel, recognized an opportunity to bring a conference to a city that had been negatively labeled and stereotyped. Well, needless to say, he ran into all kinds of frustrating situations and circumstances. I attended a meeting he held. He outlined his scope, goal, and objective, including all the key players. Consequently, things didn't fall in place, and the cooperation wasn't there, but he didn't let that stop him. (I admire his tenacity.) He took opportunity by the horns and moved his conference to a familiar and level playing ground. He didn't lose his momentum. He shook the dust off his feet and moved on.

Rather life or people, evict anxiety and frustration out of your life.

# CONCLUSION

There are those in the body of Christ who would probably not agree with me that believers don't face or have frustrations or even get frustrated. And that's all right. I want to minister and help those who are willing to admit that frustration exists and to confront it. We can't run in fear. Fear brings about three reactions: freeze, flight, and fight.

To freeze, you come to a standstill. It's a "deer staring into headlights" syndrome. It's an inescapable situation or a state of paralysis—physically, emotionally, and mentally. Peter had a freeze moment as he was warming by the fire and was asked if he were one of the disciples. He ended up denying Jesus three times.

You find yourself in flight when you run not only physically but mentally. Have you ever heard people say "My mind is racing" or "I went somewhere in my mind"? Nine times out of ten, we're running to a safe haven or a happy place. Second Kings 9:10 (AB) says, "And the dogs shall eat Jezebel in the portion of Jezreel, and none shall bury her. And he opened the door and fled." After he prophesied the aforementioned prophesy, in fear of his life, Elijah ran and hid in a cave. You find yourself fighting for your life. Your instincts kick in to survival mode.

After Pharaoh made a decree that every male child was to be killed, Exodus 2:2–3 (AB) says,

> The woman conceived and gave birth to a son; and when she saw that he was [especially] beautiful and healthy, she hid him for three months [to protect him from the Egyptians]. When she could no longer hide him, she got him a basket (chest) made of papyrus reeds

and covered it with tar and pitch [making it waterproof]. Then she put the child in it and set it among the reeds by the bank of the Nile.

What are you giving up in your fight? Is it the good fight of faith, or is it a fight out of fear?

Imagine Joseph, if you will, when he got to the palace. He had to contend daily with sexual harassment. After his constant refusal, he was falsely accused, and in addition, the evidence was stacked against him. The Bible says, even while Joseph was in prison, the favor of the Lord was with him. Everything his hands touched prospered. You may be facing frustrating times, but God's favor will remain upon you if you respond to the negativity in accordance to kingdom principles. God will continue to prosper all you put your hands to do. He'll give you double for trouble if you find yourself in a Job situation.

Let's pray.

> God, in the name of Jesus, I know you are with us to help us deal with frustration before and after deliverance. But Lord, as believers, sometimes we tend to forget that you're with us. We become fearful, which causes us to freeze, flight, or fight.

> Lord, your record speaks for itself. Your résumé of bringing your people through is extensive, and we know that there is no failure in you. You promised never to leave or forsake us. As we apply your Word, as we come in compliance with your Word, we will get the results of the Word. Thank you, Lord, for strength and power to see us through. It is you that causes us to triumph! It's a win-win! Amen!

Printed in the United States
By Bookmasters